The White Words

The
White
Words

Baron Wormser

HOUGHTON MIFFLIN COMPANY
BOSTON 1983

Library of Congress Cataloging in Publication Data

Wormser, Baron.
    The white words.

    I. Title.
PS3573.0693W5 1983   811'.54   82-12087
ISBN 0-395-33109-9
ISBN 0-395-33110-2 (pbk.)

Printed in the United States of America

P 10 9 8 7 6 5 4 3 2 1

Certain poems in this book first appeared in the following publications:

American Scholar: "Piano Lessons"; *Black Warrior Review:* "The Brothers"; *Kennebec:* "Beech Leaves" and "Cord of Birch"; *Massachusetts Review:* "Immigrant's Letter"; *MSS:* "Men"; *Poetry:* "Of Small Towns," "Servants," "A History of Photography," "The Spirit That Speaks," "Letter from New England," "The Lesser God," "Passing Significance," "A Report on the Victorians," and "Some Happiness."

For Janet

Contents

I

Passing Significance

"No one of importance here," the chief assessor
Mutters as he stamps the snow off his boots
And looks around at his fellow travelers
In the sitting room of an inn
That is the only inn thereabouts.

No one picks up his remark.
The young man in the shadows
In the far corner continues to think about
The letter he should write. Occasionally he takes
A gold watch from his coat pocket and toys with it
Absent-mindedly. An infant cries.
A woman sings softly,
A border song about flowers and stars.
In front of the fireplace sit two nuns.
The innkeeper's
Wife keeps sneezing. She wonders who will try
To sneak off without paying. A dog, at the feet
Of an old man with huge mustaches, sighs.
A clerk contentedly rustles what
Passes for a newspaper in these parts.

There are names for everyone, for every day,
And every sort of weather. There are kings
On top of kings. To study other people
You must be free and easy and remember nothing.
Then you will see what it is about each one of them
That has passing significance. There is a book somewhere.
In it are names, as beautiful as they are obscure.

Of Small Towns

It is not so much gossip that absorbs
Them as a fondness, to be found
Even in the children, for measuring lives:
The noting of how many years some wife
Has outlived her husband and how each of the road
Commissioner's four children quit high school
In the middle of the eleventh grade and how
It was twenty years to the day (they are
All addicted to anniversaries) that
A black spruce fell on a one-armed man.
Comparison is insistent — the father who
Is a better shot but not as good a card
Player as the son; the sister who
Writes poems while the other two clean house.
Here, people want to live to learn
Who the next President will be, how many
Games the World Series will go, whether
The trains will ever come back.
Ceremonious and dutiful to national symbols,
Too many of the sons die in the wars.
The coffins indicate that faraway
Places exist, that you can die quite forcibly
Elsewhere. Those who have hoisted themselves up
And fled will say that the finitude of
Small-town life breeds idiocy, that
The imagination turns upon itself, chews
Its substance over and over until it is worse
Than nothing. The surmises that the metropolis loves
To make, the crushes of people whose names you will
Never know, the expansive gestures made
Among incoherent buildings — all that is
Peculiarly urban and self-aware is lacking.
Instead you have a hodgepodge:
Legends hovering, dreams that lapse into
Manias, characters ransacked like cottages

In winter. Each random movement would become
An event. It is no surprise that every now
And then the attentiveness becomes too great
And some hamlet spawns a horror
Of the first degree. As is to be expected,
The *émancipé*'s letters home are blunt:
"You are all like those vile canning jars,
Lidded and sealed and put away for endless winter."
And yet — it is these towns that dignify the slimmest
Of lives with a history, remembering even dogs
With an earnest pleasure, a rush of anecdote and regret.

Servants

What happened to them?
The men were drafted in the war; the women
Went to live with daughters who had flats of their own;
The young ones ran off; the old ones took world tours.

What happened to them?
They lost their faith, casually, without a fuss,
Being somewhat cynical to begin with.
The master was a pederast, the mistress a glutton.
Both were insanely stingy.

What did they do?
Announced guests, changed diapers, served roasts,
Sensed desire before it was voiced,
Practiced circumspection, never yawned.

What did they do?
Soothed quarrels, offhandedly explained the basics
Of sex, walked playmates home, devised contests,
Made jam and mocked doctors, in general
Were as wise as wizards.

How big were their lives?
No more than a shoe box — a few locks
Of the children's hair, some excursion tickets, letters
From home, a good-luck charm that was never used.

How big were their lives?
They saw the world getting on and grew
Envious, read advanced novels and technical
Manuals and magazines, demanded that
Their children be sent to schools.

And we?
All the better for it, relieved of decorum
We parade around our houses in our underwear,
Disparage goblins and sprites, know how to fry eggs.

And we?
All the worse for it, cramped, robbed
Of our prerogatives and kindnesses. Without an audience
We grow shoddy, become imprecise in our speech,
Believe in the future.

Sunday Promenade

The elegance of costume varied a good deal.
Among the poor an observer could detect
Certain persistent tokens of self-respect:
The pair of shoes with new laces and heels,

The ribbon that was not greasy with use,
Brutally clean hands, the children in frocks.
The better-off encased themselves in cloth.
A new order of priests, they were fond of a ruse,

A cigar, an edifice on a quiet street
With a modest sign and leather chairs.
The throne was undergoing minor repairs;
Intelligence had been received of marching feet.

Meanwhile, this precise ritual was dutifully maintained —
The eyeing, the detailed greeting, the moral snub,
The murmur, the nod, and, afterward, the grub.
Solemn and ardent, at cutlets no man feigned.

The other days went by in a tepid dream
Of receipts, journeys at dusk, wagons of goods,
And pay. An effacement only Sunday could
Make right: "Citizens, stare! To live is to be seen."

Hegel & Co.

The eminent were found to be lacking in Mind.
History took to leaping like a dolphin
In the sea. Ideas, not paladins, would win
Whatever seemed worthwhile at the time.

The jumble of nations became a blackboard scrawl.
"A professor's vision, one who employs two maids
And dines on three grilled chops at noon each day,"
The rankled pastors sneered. In vain. The Fall

Lacked the dignity of secular proof.
Each silly auditor was a Kant of sorts.
Out went duels, in came ceaseless change —

To the rider of logic nothing was strange.
Destinies called, the Ego left its pale fort,
Replaced superstition with malleable truth.

The Virtues and Shortcomings
of a Humorous People

In both our prairies and cafés
The native intelligence revealed itself
Not in oratory, innuendo, or discontent
But in a thorough yet soft-spoken bemusement.

You had to listen and watch.
The raised eyebrow was our Socratic thrust.
The self-mocking joke became our national trust.

Wryly impotent, the bumpkin and the pundit stood
On the same low ground
And haltingly smiled for the isolate crowd.

What were events but a sort
Of indifferent autumn rain? A man went
About his business. Public life
Rested on a private agreement.

What truth there was, resided
In the anecdote's tone. The syllables must
Come out as slowly as blossoms,
The voice must be steady as a stream.

Surprises were not to our taste.
We preferred the drawl of custom,
The glancing acceptance of whatever was.
You couldn't get the best of us.

Death itself was only one more nickname
Or mock peeve, something we spoke of
But never believed.

Report on the Victorians

Heaven, along with the railroads and docks,
Prospered. They were separate endeavors but fitted together:
The eternal was the greater clock,
Commerce the mighty lever.
Meanwhile, money brought security, power, and ease.
It made a comforting sound on the collection plate.
It softened man's fate.
Death had no taste for debate;
Like a mower, the coughing disease
Would have its wasted crop. Hymn singers and tarts
Competed on the streets. Adjuration was the age's genius.
They were great ones for looking up. The piteous
Excited them; sentiment derided art;
And heaven was real, or, if not real, should have been.
It was where beauty lay with justice above
The filthy cities. It was where love
Overcame doubt. As horror impinged,
Purity became their passion.
Women's bodies were lost; conversation
Consisted of the unsaid; out of admiration
And longing there grew up a cult of the dead.
Bourgeois black was the color in fashion.
Sawdust was common in the poorer folk's bread.
Sanity was impossible, instead there was realism,
The brisk "That can't be, that will not do"
And evangelism's admonitory "Christ died for you."
Their manners were good; they reinvented schisms
And tamed the sublime.
Their music was bad; their theatre worse;
Their paintings as insipid as their taste in verse.
Condemn them? Never. They are the paradigm,
The fiend in the angelic face,
The hope in the presence of accountable disgrace.

A History of Photography

Prodigies flooded the market — the magnetic corset,
The one-twist tooth extractor, the camera.
At the exhibitions only the occasional
Yokel, up from the South, gaped in disbelief.

The church was not in principle opposed
To such a machine. Baudelaire granted its
Historical worth. Now, great-grandparents
Could be scrutinized, lost courtyards found,

Scenic postcards sent. Not great things
But something, nonetheless. A few professors
Hoped that the arrested moment might explain
To men mutability's shrewd devices.

Time would become richer, the human race
More meditative. Albums accumulated;
Robbers were apprehended by alert,
Newspaper-scanning citizens; rhetoric fizzled.

A sprinkling of adventuresome sons became
Photographers, another sort of profession,
Self-taught and self-employed. "I am not
A mechanic," more than one was forced to shout.

Reality, like a dumb beast, yawned.
You saw them with their apparatuses
Roaming the quays, the moors, the poor quarters,
The parliaments. There could be, the wits

Explained, no events without photographers.
Still, who could argue with modern life?
And for every locomotive there was
Relief to be found in some melancholic stroller,

Some Sunday morning wedding, some frolicsome
Roué. No photographer (the
Psychologists noted) had ever despaired,
Although a few had to be artists and speak

Of subtleties that embarrassed the unimproved
Eye. Yet everyone agreed that even they
Were honest sorts, content to display their illuminations
On walls, content to lap up the world like so many

Warm-tongued cats. Mom smiled, Dad winked, the camera
Whose omnipotence the reviewers found "refreshing" blinked.

II

Letter from New England

"Poor deity," murmured one of the mourners, "ever shuffling
And dealing from the same pack of cards." It was
One of those typical midwinter days,
A mirthless sun giving way to gray sky
And a minute, dry snow. The hearse was held up
For ten minutes by two dogs fighting in the street.
No one could separate them. Finally they stopped
From exhaustion. A woman — someone said she was
A cousin — began to laugh at the sight of blood
On the snow. Thompson led her down a side street.
A cardinal perched on a limb of an elm
Directly above the minister's head. After a while
It flew away. My daughter plans to write a sonnet
About it. The young may be forgiven, I suppose,
Their cravings for the emblematic. For me,
The boosting of the image has always signaled
A grasping, expedient wit.

In a Genre Studio

"This is what you will do,"
The master said, and that was how
It was, the subject came to you.
It was women with porcelain skin,
Tumultuous Biblical scenes,
Generals, and frantic equine dreams.
You daubed and tried to see
Whatever was there, whatever
There was to repeat or refine.
"There is no need for imagination.
There is a need for a firm
But not vicious shade of red,"
The master said.
And it became clear
After years of swoons and swords
That you had, in fact, got something,
However practical and plain —
That everything was something to paint.
"God's majesty lies in His indifference,"
The master said.
With time and practice you too
Began to feel at home with prolixity.
You saw the narrowness of the inner voice.
There was no wisdom in choice;
You could paint madonnas or cats
Or suburban villas or streamlined trains.
You could be discreetly reverential, calm.
"No human interest is ever worth
More than the time of day,"
The master said
As he opened a window
One genius of an afternoon
In the prime of May. "It is
This light that is everywhere
That has everything to say."

The Privilege

Oh their discussions!
They loved the word better than their God.
Discussions of arias, mineral waters, subjectivism,
The American Indian, Mendelssohn's conversion, sports
In the modern world, monetarism, astronomy:
They understood, speculated, quoted, proved.
Spiders, whatever they caught in their webs
They examined, blessed, and released.
You never realized how inexhaustible the world
Was until you spent an evening with them on
The terrace of one of those huge wooden hotels.
You didn't expect people to give you that feeling.
Usually it was the ocean or the migrating birds
Or the flowers in an upland meadow that did it,
Making you feel at once mystic and keen. The privilege
Of talking, of having thoughts, we with our hiking boots
And sketchpads overlooked until we stumbled on
These professional *Menschen*, so content with their cups
Of tea and less-than-good cigars. They had tongues!
Maybe it was because no one of importance ever
Asked them anything, or because they would never make
A decision that mattered, that they were so lively.
Maybe it was just an inclination they gave themselves
Up to happily, a habit that was centuries old.
Some of them were old, but at their talk they were
Ardent as schoolboys, refusing to be wry or shrewd.
What could happen to such lives but that they would be
Intruded upon? Whatever had the articulate to do
With the literal world? Language was embroidery.
One day the waiters and porters and clerks pounded
On their doors brandishing guns and badges, saying,
"We hate you. Soon you will babble no more."
And the conversationalists went off,
Certain that talk was its own reward.

Henry James

Each reader has his or her notion
Of what it was like. I think of the light thick
As the flesh of a pear, the ices, bells, mimicked
Taunts, and the American at his precise devotions,
    An onlooker who, even then, felt no call
    To indulge the authorial lie — knowing all.

The great Cambridge clarity became overcast;
The uptown Babel died down to a distant hum.
Europe was there waiting "to be done" —
Avaricious, lapsed, bloated with the past.
    An explorer, he enjoyed danger's charms,
    Welcomed duplicity's welcoming arms.

He stood poised between two worlds, refused to swear
An oath as to the uprightness and extent
Of his appetite. Assumptions strangled men.
He would go his way, breathe the actual air,
    Avoid the jacket of rhetoric, that stale tact
    That mystified the most trifling fact.

We admire his talent for work, his good will,
His delight in the show of life, his mannerly nerve.
"This American never gapes," a countess observed.
He admired, stewed, considered, hovered, thrilled,
    Courted the gulf that lay beneath the word,
    Let the tremor of innocence be heard.

Uncle Poetry

I had an uncle who was the only
Person in our town — which was a small town,
One funeral parlor and one set of traffic lights —
Who claimed to know all about
Tropical birds (although he had never been
South of Philadelphia), bone china,
Skeet shooting, and poetry. This uncle on
My father's side worked in the bank
And had been to college out of state.
Poets, he said, are the most ignorant of people,
Even more ignorant than politicians.
They are pleased with how things strike them,
Invite the adventitious, exclaim, rebuke strangers.
Many of them carry notebooks for the sole purpose
Of writing down their random thoughts.
Poets are sneaky people who nurse certain words
The way a nasty boy will favor a scar.
They set you up for those words, you are just
Reading along when some adjective appears.
They want you to like what they like.
They are all little dictators that way.
I suppose the world needs poets, though,
He'd say by way of ending,
And let me feel the weight of his portentous,
Breathing-through-his-nose silence.
"Uncle, you look like a dragon," I said one day,
And he never until I became a tax-paying
Citizen spoke to me concerning the muse again.

The Lesser God

Sprawled on a couch a hundred and fifty years
After the fact, sipping on a beer,
I find my sympathy comes hard
And to read these poems attentively is beyond
My means. It seems cruel that time has come so far.
The words are there, a pond
That will not be stirred, but the quickening sense,
The rhythm of thought, has been killed.
There is nothing at which to take offense;
There is nothing to affirm. All is still
And will stay still. Some pathos must
Reside in this. I am not sure, this may
Always have been dust,
Although the era adored his so-called "lays."
The frontispiece conveys a public face,
A friend to friends and a stranger to disgrace.
Yet his words, definable as they are, confuse.
Why is he so ardent to convince
And who is this much-sought-after muse?
Is he afraid the imaginary will wince
At his performance and leave him to write on alone?
Was there something for which he meant to atone?
Was his attitude toward women unfair?
Who cares?
His urgency has congealed, his politics lapsed,
His verities grown stale. My foot is asleep.
I am ashamed. Contempt for the past
Is a miserable thing. My pride will not keep
Me from this man's fate.
Perhaps it is an impertinence to open such books
At all. They have done what they intended to do.
They were not written for me and you,
They did not invite our unquiet looks.
They could say, "You are late"
And leave it at that. What is our recognition but a vice,

An excuse to digress? The content is all:
Haphazard or true, things want to be told
(Though a laden art sways and frequently falls).

The problem is that things get old.

Let the meditative move through the world unenticed.
For them the subject is a symbolic nod
To circumstance. They disavow time's topical plod.
I like my poet who perished while serving the lesser god.

Rhetoric

Traduced by recent centuries,
Archfiend to visionaries and functionalists alike,
Trove of insincerity, delusion, and vulgarity,
I find myself, however uneasily, pondering you.

Were you once better than second nature?
Did men sing in your well-wrought chains?
Was there an atmosphere you carried with you,
Blessing happenstance with logic and passion?

That you should become an outcast seems more than
Irony, you who were the oil of empire,
The centurion of language — early, classical, or
Degenerate, it was all the same to you.

Wasn't "change" yet another sharp artifice,
A way to accommodate the ungovernable?
You never believed in belief. Faced with railroads
And slums, the craven eye did you in.

It was a world stripped of altars, gods, and groves.
The word itself became a sort of nothing,
A coin, a necessity, a pet, a fact.
Even orators believed that "that was that."

All that was left was a determined spontaneity,
The mind hitting out like a fist.
But you were no good at reclaiming the unknown.
You were too artful, too mighty, too pat.

There is then it seems no place for you
In the annals of latter-day communication.
The moment has become the vehicle of annunciation,
All roads lead to reduction.

I needn't worry. You'll be back
Someday. Throngs will cheer. Impulse
Must be built upon if it is to last.
Elaboration never went fast.

A Portrait of the Artist Not As An Artist

When you're young they tell you Polonius-like
That you can't deceive yourself,
That the arras you stab must bleed,
But you believe — as much as you believe anything —
That it isn't true,
That all their telling is a snow that melts
In the sun of you.
You are your own ruse
And may do for yourself what the world won't do.
The world is a ball thrown high into
The air that does not come down.
It is where
Nothing continues and nothing is new.
It is enchanting but cruel.
You cast spells on the other neighborhood children,
Extravagantly curse, declaim, and finally write.
The words are like a confused blessing
That welcomes you and keeps you at bay.
The words are a fine irrelevance.
You live for years there in that hovering
Until the day comes when there still are days:
Your life remains unwritten.
You get tired, the way a minor god would get tired,
And ask others what they think.
Their lives are in their thighs and throats and legs.
Their speaking is a place you've never been.
They shake hands and banter and swap news.
It is enchanting.
You can't deceive yourself, what you write is you.

III

Facts of Life

It is attitude's justification that these know-
It-alls should preen themselves and submissively crow.
Reticence is thrift,
But they must make of their knowledge a gift,

For regardless of the era, weather, or *mise en scène*
The words must be spoken that somehow will befriend
A lisping fool.
The schooled must be revealed as unschooled,

The intuitive told it no longer will do.
Adulthood is where imagination must fail you,
And explanation repeal
All magic. You must think about how you feel.

It is a promise: the initiatory moments will come —
Glowering, flailing, magnificent, glum.
Someday you too
Will stand here and testify to your coming through.

"It's like this," and the revelation begins,
The word behaving as though it were a twin
To the ominous act.
It is a speech. There are no facts.

The Brothers

In the lives I liked to read as a boy there were always
Two brothers. One knew what to make of things.
His mind was full of gears. His hands were clever.
He saved up to visit the Exposition. Adults praised him.
The other brother loved horses, made up stories,
And went around barefoot. He died of smallpox
Or influenza at age twelve. It was sad but it
Was all right because he would not have become anything.
He didn't want anything to be
Any different from what it was.
I could imagine his large, milky eyes
And his wavering voice. His brother, the one who lived
And became famous, teased him. Of course he took it
Good-naturedly. That was how he was, good-natured.
In the books, the locales and hardships varied but
The brothers were always there. It seemed to have
To be that way, with one having ideas
And saying "Can't you see?" and the other
Spending afternoons in the barn
Watching swallows. It was the romance of common sense
I was reading, the new galvanic industrial
Fairy tale. I still think of them and how
No two things are equal, how one brother must seize
The sluggish day, while the other must be smote and lost.

Best Man

It was not exactly his day.
He liked that —
The approximation of joy.
Someone else was inventing a world.
No one knew what would happen.
There were inclinations, analogies, ties
That looked strong, but no one knew
Whether jelly, steel, or dust would be the result.
Nothing wrong with uncertainty, he felt,
As he brushed off his favorite old suit.
He would bless it, gladly drink to it,
Kiss it forthrightly. He would stand nearby,
An empathetic Adam, alive to the happenstance
Of things, carousing with his eyes,
Extolling this best of all worlds —
The one he freely could leave.

Pragmatic

Although his father, a balding minister,
Didn't say, it was known
That one of the places God dwelt
Was in the refrigerator coils. When things were O.K.,
God hummed, and when they weren't
He was silent as a stone.
Then you were alone.

You waited for something eternal
To occur. A breeze made
A window in its indifferently nailed
Casement tremble. How long could a boy
Hold his breath before he
Became queasy and mislaid
Whatever frayed

Talisman it was that protected him
From the commonplace?
It was thought which, like a deft kiss,
Rescued him, revealing, as it did, that intention
Might suffice, and things be reduced
To a frail handhold on space,
An exhausted face

From which shone a modest light.
For an inventor, as with that Omnipotence
He once knew, there were, in fact, no mistakes.
Time took out all the wrinkles and spots and ruts
In one philanthropic bestowal —
Here is the present tense,
The making of sense.

Piano Lessons

"The Johnsons have her and so must we":
That is how I came to know Miss Lee.
I was to play the piano, if not well
Then enough so that my mother could tell
Another mother I was taking again this year —
It was an expense, but I was a dear.
Miss Lee would coax me and I would cry.
"I can't do any better however I try;
It isn't in me," I'd say and sit down once more.
Miss Lee would motion and start to pace the floor
And we were off again, manacled to one
Another by our common sense of misfortune.
I knew it was harder for her than for me;
She had to watch as I defiled what she esteemed.
At night she played for herself alone;
But even then the music was not wholly her own,
For the neighbor boys would gather on her walk
And at some bravura passage begin to squawk,
Crow, shout, huzzah, yelp, bray,
Until she came out on her porch and they ran away.
Her talent, the town observed, kept her poor.
Once she cursed me, another time she slammed a door
And ran upstairs. I heard her rolling on her bed.
When she came down, she smiled sadly and said,
"That's enough for today." Next week came.
I loitered outside until she called my name
And I shuffled in. "Someday you will be great,"
She said, and I felt she was talking straight
Past me and into another world where
There were no clumsy fingers nor fidgety glares
At the clock on the wall nor hectoring half-notes
Nor folded dollar bills. I took off my coat,
And we walked into the room where the piano stood
For all that we wanted to do yet never would.

Child's Play

The lawn is America,
The sagging wicker chair a throne,
The out-of-bloom lilacs are waves,
It is raining pine cones.

Far off the indulgent smiles
Of the grownups.
They are clever.
Their tea dives into their cups.

They see what is there,
Belittle what is not.
Sentinels whose senses are tombs,
They do not hear
The excitement upstairs,
The roar in the next room.

Abundance annoys them, charged
As they are with the duty
Of tidying up so many years.

They cannot stop in their tracks
And gaze. They know, they know.
Ten thousand suns and moons
Have told them so.

When they stoop and pretend
To give themselves up
To the game at hand
It only makes things worse.
They collapse and wrinkle,
Coax the hapless,
Vex the adept,
Ask questions,
Invent new rules,

Finally rise, head shaking,
Bones creaking, to say,
"So this is what you do,"
And look around a bit
Anxiously to make sure
In the meantime their own kind
Has not disappeared.

The Light Child
for Owen

This tender certainty sits lightly as
A good king's mantle. Like calls to like:
The game of marbles, the wooden plane
That flies ten feet and descends to earth,
The cocoon on the garden fence. What is
Learned is what wants to be learned, is bidden
By the leaping mind. Fascination is homely,
Pockets are to be filled, and exclamations
Actual. Even the tears that disrupt
A moment are proper, showing as they do
That there is no shield between alacrity
And rough matter. A fall is a fall — a grievous
Yet soon diminished fact, a misstep amongst
An untamed abundance. Things will happen;
There is much to purely do. His day is a dawn.

Some Happiness
for Maisie

I tell my daughter about this pitfall
And that difficulty.
She listens, but it is hard
For her to be patient.
With a kiss, I dismiss her
And she dismisses me.

She is happy. I pick at that
Commonly discredited fact.
It is something I had not thought of,
That love might have this humming, incautious outcome,
That a daughter could be like the sea
In the rain, absorbing the many drops.

She is
All things that steadily, waveringly go.

I am on the shore, kicking at what I know.

There is a day without conclusions.
There is a word without weight.
There is an impulse familiar as skin.

I lay my perils down.
Childhood is a string tied
To a great, remarkable nothing.

We dance
To a music beyond misgiving.

Description

As a boy, I was afraid of big dogs, electrical storms,
And novelists. A novelist might see me and describe me:
"A small, freckled boy, afraid of big dogs, he walked as if
The earth beneath him were made of eggshells." That would have
    been it
For me; I was described — unfairly, of course, as all descriptions
Were unfair, but possessing, as all descriptions did, a facility
That was as good as accuracy.
"Oh him!" people would have said. "There is no mystery in him."
At my best I might have embodied some materialistic force — fear
Or the foolishness of freckles. How sordidly I was being used,
The gleam and shadow of my days cashed in for the ease
Of a few words! I prepared a speech, in it
I would say, "Reject this evil limitation, this incisive pomp.
Even a boy is not a bug but a clamorous uncertainty,
A leapfrogging possibility. Let me go unknown and you will be
Rewarded." Rehearse such talk as I did, I never used it.
Let them come to me now and say,
"A man of average build, his eyes betrayed
A certain apprehensiveness, as if some habitual secret
Resided therein."
I would say without a twinge, "Yes, that is him."

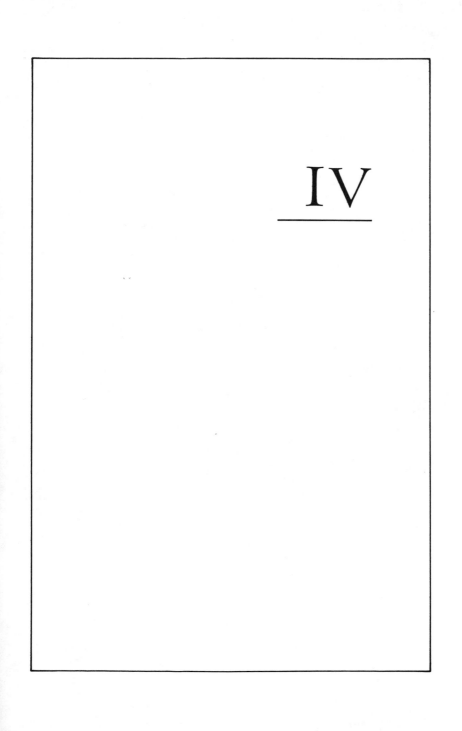

IV

The White Words

Words, it turned out, were
White but not to be contemned.
The streets of Baltimore, the novels
Of Trollope, the future of my sister:
All topics contained the lulling rhythm
That was talk, wave upon graceful
And laborious wave. For a time the toil
Of pain would disperse. In my mother's eyes
A startled serenity would appear. Morphine
Was forgotten, and I wanted to be a wooden
Thing, a half-human marionette capable
Of talking forever, a brave body hoping
To coax from that puffy blotched face
A smile, however bewildered and slow.
Applaud life. I wore down,
My tongue became heavy and thick.
The very air seemed sickly.
Two tired strangers, we looked about
Distractedly for that spot where
The white words still hovered.

The Blind Man

All time becomes a night as long as
A prairie. A man who shuffles and pauses and sniffs
The air like a woodchuck will never cross it.
He combs his hair until his woman says
"Stop. You look fine." He smiles at her voice,
And when he is gone she tells her friends about
His characteristics, about the way he talks about
Himself in the third person as if he were
Someone else. He has tried to explain that.
There are distances, he has said, that you have not
Considered. Your vision is a mouth. You have
Lived as a prodigal. For me, between the finger
And the hand and the arm and the head
There are distances. Slowly he would lift an arm,
More slowly than the marionettes she remembered
From her childhood. It is remarkable, he has said
With that smile, that I am not weary.
His hands are what she loves most.
They are soft and, at once, tentative and sure.
No one could caress her the way the blind man does.
The hands are reverent and move without haste.
There is time.

Cord of Birch

It was high summer, that time when winter seems
Implausible, a moralist's admonitory dream,
That I, short-sleeved, took through the neighborhood
A question, revealing it only when it was understood
All round that the amenities as to the heat and flies
Had been upheld, when something like response might thrive.
A hundred sixty years of working in the woods,
Their lives were sure to contain the fact or two
I wanted about some birch I'd cut that spring
And the extent of its aptitude for making heat.
To a man they grunted — that to let me know they knew
That I was bothering about a very poor thing.
I relaxed in the shade of their attitude,
Ignorant that each was to recall, surmise, delete,
And say that which the others had said was untrue.
Gravely I agreed with their unblinking contrarieties.
My hand shook hands and the doubt inside me
Hurrahed. Back home there was the cord, a pile
I'd left beside the back path. I pouted awhile,
Hefted a piece — it was wood. Nothing descended.
At night in bed I defined and mused and pretended;
Nothing came of it all but dismal sleep.
By New Year's the snow was over two feet deep;
Load by load my dilemma was taken away,
And often I stopped to stare on my way
Back from the shed at the smoke the fire had freed
And let myself be gratified by the wisdom of need.

Beech Leaves

It's hard to ignore them. The winter woods,
    Niggardly as a modernist painting,
Abet them. There are no restful blurs.
    You can see past everything

To those saplings whose leaves, though slightly curled
    And almost transparent, are all still there.
The settlers (books say) stuffed pillows with them,
    Thus refuting the devil's eiderdown snares.

Their delicacy surprises. How is it they've gotten away
    With being indifferent to all skeletal pride?
One might suspect that these dead
    But clinging leaves were in touch with something denied

By all other categorizable cells,
    Had mastered some Pharaoh's strategies,
Consulted one of the more idiosyncratic
    Holy books. They rattle in the breeze.

I thrash amid reverie's false depths
    Until a raven commences to caw.
A mocker and a reminder of the baser facts,
    I must agree with it that there are laws,

That it's only January that lends these leaves
    A mantle of invincibility.
Men and ravens know another season
    Is coming when beech leaves will part meekly

To become part of that undistinguished
    Duff hidden beneath the snow.
Let there be ends. This lingering is for now.
    These leaves, like men, will cling to what they know.

A Later Death

She'd been depressed, is what the papers said.
In her photo she gazes out, pretty and pert.
It's hard to imagine her being dead,
Much less her killing herself. One who'd been bred
For other things, there seemed in her no home for hurt.
She'd been depressed, is what the papers said.
Her mother believed it came from what she'd read
About the Jews. She'd become strangely alert —
It's hard to imagine her being dead —
To the slightest things. Those Jews and their deaths spread
A net over her, their torment was her shirt.
She'd been depressed, is what the papers said:
She wished to lie down in the Jews' ruined bed,
She wished to touch their flesh that had turned to dirt.
It's hard to imagine her being dead
Who for so long had been a stranger to dread
And care. Like history she grew pale and curt.
She'd been depressed, is what the papers said.
It's hard to imagine her being dead.

Men

TO THE MEMORY OF LOUISE BOGAN

Men perch on mountains in their minds.
Across chasms they roar.
No sound returns. Their thoughts are hard thoughts.
Their lives go for war.

They do not stay at the window
For the last crumbs of light.
They do not hear the doves whom
The dawn wind incites.

They swagger when they should be mindful and still,
They clutch when they should relent.
They speak to provoke, and after the fact
Explain what they meant.

They cannot bother with commonplace truths,
With stitches or spoonfuls or quilts.
They abrade love until it is a powder
Of pleasure and guilt.

Whoever would live with them they subdue,
Saying, "That is our way."
All life endangers them. What they cannot
Arrest, they betray.

Private

"The pay is good" — that's the sort
Of thing the enlistees commonly say,
Although they tend to look away
When they reply. Being in forts
Was something one thought of doing when one
Was little. Now grown up to a size-
Twelve boot, one holds an actual gun
And salutes each inauspicious sunrise.

If only the sun never rose
And the women didn't figure out
That a soldier was a kind of lout
With chipped teeth and broken nose.
Some say it's being told what to do
That befuddles the men the most.
There is an ideology to lacing your shoes.
When they give you a day to go to the coast

In a bus and your civilian clothes
Things rarely ever go quite right.
For one, you've got to be back by night
And the skirts all seem to know
You aren't a candidate, that you've sold
Yourself cheap. So you drink beers, throw
The bottles at signs, try out the holds

They've taught you in martial-arts class
On buddies who've had one or two more beers
Than you. To the baseguards it's "Cheers!"
As you rub your groin and roll your ass.
In a cold bed your body throbs.
Your braggart father's in your sleep;
Your mother grabs at you and sobs.
A woman laughs; the stalking light leaps.

Some Recollections Concerning the
Exiled Revolutionary, Leon Trotsky

From the way people used to bother him,
Or tried to bother him, you would have thought
He had the millenium in his back pocket.
"I am becoming a doctor," he used to say and wince.
Wherever you looked there was some reminiscence
By someone who had met him for an hour.
For each person he was a lens.
Why be a man or woman if you can be
A personality? It's much easier.
Looking over all the press clippings, we thought
It was surprising that he was a man at all.
Indeed he must have wondered what role he was
Playing, the censored guest of this or that
Nervous regime. No other nation, it seemed,
Wanted to be reinvented. Afflicted with brilliance
He went on thinking, when a simpler man
Could see that the quiddities had been left behind.
He went on talking — as light began to come
Into the room and voices were heard in the streets —
As if his words could obliterate the telltale day.
Behind his back we called him Prospero.
He had been so close to heaven — bloody
A heaven as it was — and had not entered.
You could see the torment of this in his eyes: "I have
Lived on earth as only a handful of men have
Ever lived. My thoughts have stood and walked.
Friends and enemies have died . . ."
His wife bustled around. Some old comrade remarked
About how ideology and vituperation were inseparable.
The road to paradise was paved with blackened reputations.
Each hero must have a dupe.
I can see him scolding someone's dog for misbehaving,
I can hear his voice — strident, sure, enslaved.

Immigrant's Letter

Everyone thinks they know what it is like here.
The ones who were born here know because they have
Always been here. It is their home and they can tell
When something is out of place. The ones who came here
Know because they have had to learn everything. Study
Has made them practiced observers. I, however,
Know nothing of this place. In this I do not mean to complain
Or play the fool. It's true that I didn't know what
I was getting myself into, but I did know what I
Was leaving. Work for nothing back there, die like
A plow horse. I knew what I was leaving. Here you can sit
All day and no one says anything to you about it.
It's assumed that you are thinking. It is a courtesy
I appreciate, but they are such an unelaborate people.
It is like a big, easy-going army. Is that it?
Everyone gives himself a task. There is a sort of general
In a business suit at the top. He smiles but is stern.
All you have to do is want what everyone else wants,
And you belong here. It doesn't matter how much
You possess — you would not believe what "rich" means here —
It's the wanting that helps everyone get along.
Even when you get old and die, you still want.
It is like a parade. What I wouldn't give for one
Of their cars! All I would do would be to drive around.
My ass would get soft, my fingers would grow around
The steering wheel. As it is, all I have are sunglasses.
You cannot see me in them. I become like a fish
In them, or a magician. I am sending no
Money home this letter. I know nothing.

Eine Neue Fabrik, 1912

It is the pallor of the place that surprises most,
As if the brave new world had caught a cold.
One wonders what they made of it even back then:
Did the newspapers speak respectfully
Of a bridge between metaphor and money,
Of an industrialist's shrewd caprice,
Of a botched democracy's inadvertent showpiece?
It doesn't matter;
Motive has collapsed along with the roof.
Their vision has become a quotation,
Their dynamism so much wheezy naiveté.
The guard — this is not a Gothic ruin,
Iron is redeemable — fusses over a hotplate,
Leaving us to wander about and imagine
The placards, the noise, and the workers, brisk
And attentive, chewing all the while on the word *class*.
They embraced what destroyed them.
That's usually the case. Locust trees
Hide the shattered windows, the shell
Of a generator squats like a wrestler
On the cracking cement floor.
It is people, not machines, who anguish.
We inheritors finger glass, curse, laugh,
Finally in the stark late-afternoon light
Confess our own frozen hopes
Amid this rubble of efficient days.

The Spirit That Speaks

The spirit that speaks in the iris
Exclaiming at length a poise of blossom
Is not spirit but laborious congruence,
A stiff dance, the shy shop girl
Falling in love with a handsome stranger.
A credulous event, too minute
To represent that reductive will invoked
By unnerved lecturers; an enterprise, not an answer,
With no goal unless repetition were a goal,
Feet moving because they were feet,
Possibility like a child leery of water
Waddling eon-slow toward the edge
Of the pond of being. Remove the iris and the world
Goes, a zeppelin ripped and plummeting,
All the industrious captains staring out
The widening portholes, wondering for the first time,
As birds and baggage fly by, if
Existence is, after all, a passive tumult,
An unprincipled verb, a blindman's certainty.
All this, and more, is what the iris would not tell me.

Nothing But

In this book there is a story
That starts like an owl's hoot
On a winter night —
Nothing but sound running through
Cold air, then quiet
As if an owl were never there.
To hell with the pathos of volition:
This story is better than that.
Instead of a thought, there is a place —
It doesn't matter whether it's a room
Or a forest or a mineface.
It only matters that it is, so to speak,
A long place — where water is
Slowly dripping in a tunnel
Or where there are roots or walls
Or breezes that have no outcome.
There is, in this story, a sky without planes,
Nothing but clouds and a shade of blue.
There is a pause that is
Like a god's pitying gaze.
Then some people appear.
They will enact the drama of words,
And in what has become a background
There will persist a swelling sound that
Is majestic, but in this story is like a heartbeat,
Is something too real to ever quite be heard.